Looking at Life Cycles

Frog

Victoria Huseby

Smart Apple Media

Smart Apple Media is published by Black Rabbit Books
P.O. Box 3263, Mankato, Minnesota 56002

Printed in the United States

Published by arrangement with the Watts Publishing Group Ltd, London.

Editor: Rachel Tonkin
Designer: Proof Books
Illustrator: John Alston
Picture researcher: Diana Morris
Science consultant: Andrew Solway
Literacy consultant: Gill Matthews

Picture credits:
Jane Burton/Nature PL: 11; Chinch Gryneiwicz/Ecoscene: 5;
Mike Maidment/Ecoscene: 1, 19; Neil Miller/Ecoscene: 9;
Robert Pickett/Ecoscene: front cover, 7, 13, 15, 17;
Robin Redfern/Ecoscene: 21

Library of Congress Cataloging-in-Publication Data

Huseby, Victoria.
        Frog / by Victoria Huseby.
        p. cm.—(Smart Apple Media. Looking at life cycles)
        Summary: "An introduction to the life cycle of a frog, from egg to adult"—
Provided by publisher.
        Includes index.
        ISBN 978-1-59920-176-4
        1. Frogs—Life cycles—Juvenile literature. I. Title.
QL668.E2H87 2009
597.8'9—dc22
                                                                                2007030463

9 8 7 6 5 4 3 2 1

Contents

Laying Eggs

In spring, a female
frog lays lots of **eggs** in
a pond. The eggs are soft
and stick together to
make **frog spawn**.

Inside the Eggs

The frog spawn floats to
the top of the water. Inside
each egg, a baby frog is
growing. Each egg is kept
safe in a ball of jelly.

7

Hatching

A baby frog is called a
tadpole. After a few
days, the tadpole hatches
from its egg. It lives
under the water.

9

Tadpole

The young tadpole breathes
through **gills** on the side
of its head. The tadpole
eats tiny plants and small
animals in the water.

Back Legs

When the tadpole is about seven weeks old, its back legs begin to grow. Its tail begins to shrink. Its gills are now tucked inside the skin.

Front Legs

After nine weeks, a tadpole's front legs grow. It now uses **lungs** inside its body to breathe. The tadpole swims to the surface of the water to get air.

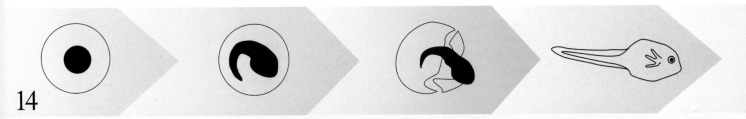

Froglet

After 12 weeks, the tadpole has become a young frog, called a **froglet**. It can live on land and in water. Soon it will lose its tail.

Adult Frog

The froglet becomes an adult
frog. It eats insects, worms,
and slugs to help it grow.
In winter, the frog **hibernates**
at the bottom of a pond.

Mating

In spring, the frog finds another frog to **mate** with. The female frog now lays lots of eggs of her own.

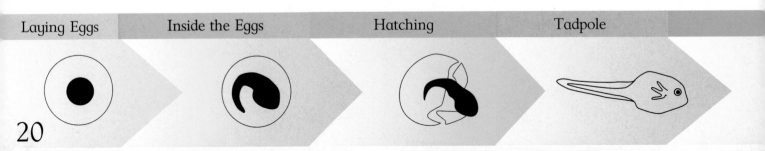

Laying Eggs   Inside the Eggs   Hatching   Tadpole

| Back Legs | Front Legs | Froglet | Adult Frog |

21

Frog Facts

- Frogs lay between 3,000 and 4,000 eggs at any one time.

- Frogs do not need to drink because they take in water through their skin.

- Most frogs have webbed feet to help them swim. Webbed feet means they have extra skin between their toes.

- The male frog sings, or croaks, to attract a female frog to mate with.

- Frogs' tongues are sticky to help them catch insects to eat.

- Frogs do not live just near water. Some frogs live underground or even in trees.

Glossary

Eggs
A baby frog grows inside an egg. Frogs' eggs are round.

Froglet
The stage between tadpole and adult frog.

Frog spawn
A large number of frog eggs stuck together in a jellylike coating that keeps them safe.

Gills
A body part that lets tadpoles breathe underwater.

Hibernate
To sleep through the winter.

Lungs
The organs in the chest that humans and many other animals use to breathe air.

Mate
When a male and female frog come together to make baby frogs.

Tadpole
A baby frog. Tadpoles have long tails and live in water.

23

Index and Web Sites

For Kids:

Animal Life Cycles
http://www.kidzone.ws/animals/lifecycle.htm

Frog Life Cycle Craft
http://www.dltk-kids.com/animals/
  mfroglifecycle.htm

Life Cycle of Frogs
http://www.tooter4kids.com/Frogs/
  life_cycle_of_frogs.htm

For Teachers:

A to Z Teacher Stuff: Life Cycles
http://atozteacherstuff.com/Themes/Life_Cycles/

**U.S. National Park Service—
Curriculum Guides**
http://www.nps.gov/cany/forteachers/
  2ndgrade.htm